My Journey Through

ELLIS ISLAND

By Lynda Arnéz

Please visit our website, www.garethstevens.com. For a free color catalog of all our high-quality books, call toll free 1-800-542-2595 or fax 1-877-542-2596.

Library of Congress Cataloging-in-Publication Data

Arnéz, Lynda.
My journey through Ellis Island / Lynda Arnéz.
    pages cm — (My place in history)
 Includes index.
ISBN 978-1-4824-4009-6 (pbk.)
ISBN 978-1-4824-3999-1 (6 pack)
ISBN 978-1-4824-4000-3 (library binding)
1. Ellis Island Immigration Station (N.Y. and N.J.)—Juvenile literature. 2. Ellis Island (N.J. and N.Y.)—History—Juvenile literature. 3. United States—Emigration and immigration—Juvenile literature. I. Title.
 JV6484.A75 2016
 304.8'73—dc23

                                    2015032505

First Edition

Published in 2016 by
Gareth Stevens Publishing
111 East 14th Street, Suite 349
New York, NY 10003

Copyright © 2016 Gareth Stevens Publishing

Designer: Laura Bowen
Editor: Kristen Nelson

Photo credits: Cover, p. 1 (immigrants) Lewis W. Hine/Museum of the City of New York/Archive Photos/Getty Images; cover, pp. 1–24 (torn strip) barbaliss/Shutterstock.com; cover, pp. 1–24 (photo frame) Davor Ratkovic/Shutterstock.com; cover, pp. 1–24 (white paper) HABRDA/Shutterstock.com; cover, pp. 1–24 (parchment) M. Unal Ozmen/Shutterstock.com; cover, pp. 1–24 (textured edge) saki80/Shutterstock.com; cover (background) Natalia Sheinkin/Shutterstock.com; pp. 1–24 (paper background) Kostenko Maxim/Shutterstock.com; p. 5 Popperfoto/Getty Images; p. 7 (Statue of Liberty) Matej Hudovernik/Shutterstock.com; p. 9 (main) iofoto/Shutterstock.com; pp. 9 (inset), 13 (main) Everett Historical/ Shutterstock.com; p. 11 (main) Universal History Archive/Universal Images Group/Getty Images; pp. 11 (inset), 17 ullstein bild/Getty Images; p. 13 (inset) Edwin Levick/Wikimedia Commons; p. 15 Fotosearch/Archive Photos/Getty 1mages; p. 19 MPI/Stringer/Archive Photos/Getty Images; p. 20 magmarcz/Shutterstock.com; p. 21 (Berlin) File Upload Bot (Magnus Manske)/Wikimedia Commons; p. 21 (Capra) Wikiwatcher1/Wikimedia Commons; p. 21 (Hope) Alex:D/ Wikimedia Commons; p. 21 (Lugosi) EeuHP/Wikimedia Commons; p. 21 (Sikorsky) Materialscientist/Wikimedia Commons; p. 21 (Boiardi) Bwmoll3/Wikimedia Commons;

Printed in the United States of America

CPSIA compliance information: Batch #CW16GS: For further information contact Gareth Stevens, New York, New York at 1-800-542-2595.

CONTENTS

Words in the glossary appear in **bold** type the first time they are used in the text.

The Long JOURNEY

September 3, 1902

   I'm very hungry. When we boarded this ship back home in Ireland, my mother and I were told we'd be given food every day. But our trip was only supposed to be about 2 months long—and it's been 2 more weeks than that! We've been told there's not enough food for everyone now. Still, I know we're getting close to land!

   My father left for America 3 years ago with my uncle. Finally, he sent us a letter with two tickets to join him there!

Notes from History

Ellis Island was the major place **immigrants** passed through to enter the United States from 1892 to 1924. It was open until 1954.

Many immigrants came to the United States for the promise of more land and better work than found in their home countries. Others wanted the freedoms given to American citizens, such as the ability to practice any faith.

Lady LIBERTY

September 5, 1902

We can see the Statue of Liberty! Even those of us who have been packed into **steerage** were able to come onto the deck to see it. My mother started crying as soon as it came into view. She told me the statue **represents** freedom for our family.

We're gathering our belongings since we'll be getting off the ship soon. I won't be sad to leave our ship room behind. So many people were seasick, it was hot, and now it smells terrible!

Notes from History

A poem on the Statue of Liberty welcomes immigrants: "Give me your tired, your poor, your **huddled** masses **yearning** to breathe free."

Ellis Island is located in sight of the Statue of Liberty in Upper New York Bay between New York City's island of Manhattan and the coast of New Jersey.

Canada

ME

VT

NH

NY

MA

CT RI

PA

Statue of Liberty
and
Ellis Island

NJ

MD

DE

WV

VA

Atlantic Ocean

7

Hurry Up AND WAIT

September 6, 1902

    We waited all night to get off the ship. It was cold, and I hardly slept. Mother and I took the first **ferry** from the ship, but there are still a lot of people waiting. Father's letter prepared us for this. He also wrote that we would have to be checked by doctors and answer questions before we met him.

    Once we reached Ellis Island, Mother and I dropped our few bags in a big room. I hope we'll be able to find them later!

Notes from History

First-class and second-class passengers were **screened** aboard their ship. It was believed that those who could afford a better ticket needed only a short doctor's **inspection** and questioning.

Depending on the number of steerage passengers, some might wait days before they were transported to Ellis Island.

Women and CHILDREN

I saw older boys and men hugging their wives and mothers—and going to a different line! I felt so sad that they had to leave their families. I'm glad I can stay with my mother!

Behind us in this big line are a girl and her brothers who were in the same ship room with us. Their parents came over from Ireland last year and sent for them a few months ago. I think they're really brave.

Notes from History

The 1891 Immigration Act stated that children without someone to care for them wouldn't be allowed into the country. Quickly, organizations formed to help those with no family come to America.

For immigrants who had all the papers they needed and no health problems, inspection at Ellis Island took about 3 to 5 hours.

Clean Bill
OF HEALTH

Mother got very thin on the trip from Ireland to America. Sometimes, she would give me some of her food and tell me to keep growing! When I started to see doctors come around the big hall, I worried they might take her away. I heard someone near us talking about a hospital on the island!

Luckily, Mother and I were considered healthy enough. I've seen other boys and girls get taken away from their mothers today, crying as they go. I hope they get better.

Notes from History

Immigrants who looked like they had common health problems were marked with a code in chalk. For example, an "H" meant heart problems.

ELLIS ISLAND HOSPITAL

Immigrants arriving with **contagious** illnesses weren't allowed to come into the United States. Some were taken to a hospital so they could be properly cared for.

13

Questions AND ANSWERS

Before we got on the ship in Ireland, Mother had to answer a list of questions. In his letter, Father told her to answer truthfully and that she'd be asked them again in America. They'd check the two lists of answers against one another.

The man who asked Mother the questions was very kind to us. He wanted to know where we were from, if we could read and write, and where we were going. There were a lot of questions!

Notes from History

Any immigrant found to have a **criminal** background wasn't granted entry into the United States.

All immigrants were asked if they had enough money for a train ticket.
In 1909, a law said all immigrants had to have at least $20 with them
when they arrived.

Entering AMERICA

It's official—Mother and I are staying in America! We had to show a letter from Father saying he would be meeting us to take us to our new home. I'm glad Father knew we needed it. Other mothers we met today have to wait in **detention** with their children until they can show they'll be going to family in the United States.

Now we just have to find our bags in that big room. I hope no one took mine.

Notes from History

Immigrants who didn't pass the doctor's inspection or the questioning at Ellis Island would be deported, or sent back to the country they came from. This didn't happen often.

If a child had a contagious disease and was deported, often one parent had to go back with them. Ellis Island was sometimes called the "island of tears."

REUNITED!

As we walked down the stairs from our inspections, I spotted Father! Father and Mother looked so happy to be together again.

Father immediately started telling us about the Irish neighborhood he and Uncle Colin lived in. For a while, they had shared rooms with several men, but now had a small apartment of their own. Father said they were saving money to build a farm out west. The United States is so big—there are so many places we could go!

Notes from History

The "kissing post" was a wooden post near the exit of Ellis Island where people hugged and kissed the family and friends meeting them after their journey to the United States.

Many immigrants stayed in the places where they arrived. Living conditions often weren't very good and jobs were hard to find.

A new HOME

Father, Mother, and I are taking another ferry to Manhattan. Father says our new home isn't too far from there. I'm going to start school, and Mother says she's going to start taking in sewing. We're all going to have to help out at home so we can make a good life for ourselves here, Father says.

I can see the Statue of Liberty from the deck of the ferry. I don't think I'll ever forget when I saw her for the first time!

Notes from History

About 12 million immigrants came through Ellis Island between 1892 and 1954.

Famous Ellis Island Immigrants

Irving Berlin
country: Russia
arrived: 1893
job: writing music

Frank Capra
country: Italy
arrived: 1903
job: movie director

Bob Hope
country: England
arrived: 1908
job: actor

Bela Lugosi
country: Hungary
arrived: 1921
job: actor

Igor Sikorsky
country: Russia
arrived: 1919
job: inventor

Ettore "Chef" Boiardi
country: Italy
arrived: 1914
job: chef and businessman

GLOSSARY

contagious: able to be passed from one person or animal to another

criminal: having to do with crime or illegal activities

detention: a place where people are held for a time until certain conditions are met

ferry: a boat used to carry passengers or goods

huddled: crowded together

immigrant: one who comes to a country to settle there

inspection: the act of looking at something closely for problems

represent: to stand for

screen: to check over closely to decide if something or someone is suitable for a place

steerage: the part of a ship where the passengers with the cheapest tickets stay

yearning: longing

For more INFORMATION

Books

Kravitz, Danny. *In the Shadow of Lady Liberty: Immigrant Stories from Ellis Island.* North Mankato, MN: Capstone Press, 2016.

Merrick, Caitlin, and Gillian Houghton. *A Primary Source Investigation of Ellis Island.* New York, NY: Rosen Publishing, 2015.

Thompson, Linda. *Immigrants to America.* Vero Beach, FL: Rourke Educational Media, 2013.

Websites

Interactive Tour of Ellis Island
teacher.scholastic.com/activities/immigration/tour/
Explore Ellis Island right from your computer screen.

Learning Adventures in Citizenship
www.pbs.org/wnet/newyork//laic/episode4/topic2/e4_topic2.html
Learn more about Ellis Island and do an activity about what you've read.

INDEX